How To Be A Fred

THOMAS YUSCHAK

Published by CreateSpace Independent Publishing Platform

ISBN-13: 978-1481160100
ISBN-10: 1481160109

Contents

Part 1: Background

Part 2: How to be Extraordinary

Part 3: How to be Extraordinary Under Pressure

Part 4: How to be Extraordinary with no Job Security

Part 5: Wrap Up

Part 1

Background

Chapter 1

Introduction

I was less than receptive when I first read the Fred factor. In its own way it added a little extra pressure to an already high pressure situation. The book had been distributed to the entire company during a period of prolonged crises and at first, it seemed to be asking even more from an already stretched group of individuals. The fact was, we were already a team of Freds, highly motivated overachievers, but had been working our hardest for months and months on end and were starting to burn out.

One afternoon late in the year, I came to my office towards the end of another emotionally exhausting day. What a year it had been so far. I was working for a small technology start-up company that was on the verge of either great success or total failure and there seemed to be no middle ground to rest upon. We had experienced a major setback early in the year and had been struggling for nine months to regain the trust and support of our partners.

To know the depth of our challenge, you must understand that our company was not yet selling any products in the marketplace. This meant there was no revenue stream to support us. Instead we had raised a limited supply of capitol to survive on until we became cash positive. To become cash positive however, required that we overcome numerous technical and manufacturing challenges and be able to clearly demonstrate that our new technology could become a commercial reality. It was only this kind of success that could unlock the market and allow our products to be sold. But because of numerous delays and what seemed to be a constant onslaught of unforeseen challenges; we were running out of cash and time much faster than we had anticipated. In order to raise new capital, we would need significant and demonstrated success; but success seemed hard for us find.

After months of uncomfortably intense scrutiny, skepticism, and occasional harsh shouting by our partners, we had finally received the approval to move forward with a second attempt of the technology that had failed earlier in the year. The whole process was messy. Not only did we have to develop a new technology, but we also had to develop new and complex manufacturing methods to be able to build it. Both were extremely challenging in their own right but when combined, represented the high risk, high potential payoff that defined us. Previous mis-steps had caused months of delays and millions of dollars in unbudgeted spend. As painful as that was, we were now in an entirely different situation. There would be no more next times. A mistake now would quickly end the program and open up the very real possibility that people would lose their jobs or even that the entire company would collapse into the memories of a lost decade. Today was the day it appeared that such a mistake had taken place. It was morning when I learned of a problem that might shut down the program. I felt my stomach sink and then rise to the center of my throat. Our partners were made aware of the situation and the questions and accusations were starting to come. It was on this day I went to my office and found a copy of the "The Fred Factor" by Mark Sanborn placed in the mailbox just outside my office door.

Over the next few days I scanned the first part of the book and to be honest, with everything we were going through, it seemed a bit naive. Fred, the perfect mailman did little to motivate me or my team. I was surrounded by people who were used to going the extra mile; by people who had excelled throughout their lifetime, who were used to doing things that "couldn't be done"; who were giving everything they had to give and had been doing so, relentlessly for a long time. This team represented everything that Fred represented and more: excellent people skills combined with excellent technical skills combined with a pure desire to go beyond normal expectations. We were driven by a passion to do our best and achieve something that had never been achieved before. But instead of lifting us up; instead of "turning the ordinary into the extraordinary"; it was wearing us down; exhausting us and raising doubts about our abilities and our future. Why? Because of a prolonged high pressure situation combined with practically no job security.

It wasn't until a few weeks later, after this great team had successfully triumphed over what seemed to be another impossible challenge, after one more hard fought step closer to the finish line, that I took another look at the Fred Factor. This time I took away two core messages:

i.   Don't settle for mediocrity in your life or in your work. You can excel in life by consciously going beyond the status quo; by caring enough to do more than the minimum; by consistently taking things to a higher level. Although most of the book focused on doing these things through interpersonal relationships, the message remains the same when applied to the technical aspects of our work and life as well.

ii.   If you succeed in doing (i), you'll be a happier, more fulfilled person in life and work.

For most of my life, these messages had rung tried and true, but now I found myself in a situation where the second part was no longer guaranteed. Not only had I found myself slipping into this situation, but I was also witnessing other Freds around me slip into it as well. I realized we were in this predicament because of the long time period we had been working under extremely challenging conditions. This was a high stakes, high profile game we were in. For us, winning didn't mean success, it meant survival to fight another day; one more battle in a war most start-up companies have to wage. More than anything, I wanted to find a way to bring the happiness, satisfaction, and personal fulfillment of a job well done back into my life and into the lives of those around me. This became my personal motivation and the motivation behind this book.

How do you be the best you can be when you're working under prolonged periods of high pressure? How do you be the best you can be when you might lose your job regardless of whether or not you achieve personal success at work? To put it more bluntly, how do you be a Fred when your work is stressing you out? Unfortunately, if you're stressed, you're not Fred.

If you're working under high levels of stress for long periods, the first part of Fred that will disappear will be the satisfaction you get from doing the best job you're capable of doing. If the stress continues on, Fred will disintegrate altogether and you'll find you can no longer go the extra mile. Mediocrity will set in and for those of us who are naturally Fred-like, dissatisfaction with ourselves or perhaps even depression will follow.

Sometimes we can make a great effort and ignore our stress for what seems like an extraordinarily long period of time but unless the stress is removed, or at least reduced to a manageable level, even the best of us will eventually burn out. When this happens our level of satisfaction, as well as the level of happiness we bring with us to work and potentially to home as well, will suffer.

There is however a difference between stress and pressure and between stress and no job security. People can be extraordinary under pressure; people can be extraordinary with no security. To do so we must recognize the pressure we're under and not allow that pressure to degenerate into stress. We probably don't have direct control of the pressure in our lives. We probably don't have the capability to lower the stakes of the work we do, nor will we be able to make an unstable company suddenly become stable. But we can limit the ability of the pressure we're under to transform into stress and by doing so, allow ourselves to excel even under the highest pressure situations or the least certain circumstances.

Chapter 2

Remembering Fred

The book the Fred Factor was written in 2004 by Mark Sanborn, whom I have never met. The story is based on the personal experience of the author with a postman (named Fred) who consistently went out of his way to do the best job he could do. The author used Fred's work ethic to form guiding principles that if followed, would allow anyone to become a "Fred". The author believed that by following these principles, a person could enrich their lives and develop a more satisfying and rewarding work experience.

He describes the importance of intending to make a positive difference every day through the power of random acts, of being committed to the people in our lives, and of acting on great ideas. Mr. Sanborn asks, "How can we change ordinary actions into extraordinary ones?", and then lays out strategies for doing so. He points out the importance of building success one relationship at a time and goes into detail about seven skills associated with relationship building: be real; be interested; be a better listener; be empathic; be honest; be helpful; be prompt.

Mr. Sanborn then describes how to continually create value for others by being enthusiastic and adding enjoyment to someone's day. He discusses why making people wait, supplying finished work with defects, and making avoidable mistakes can take value away. The author suggests that value is added by solving mistakes you didn't make, removing the frustration of others, and providing accurate information. The extraordinary employee strives to simplify the work of others and does things uncommonly well.

The Fred Factor describes how to reinvent ourselves regularly by proactively increasing our capabilities, learning from past lessons, acting on good ideas, and learning from others then taking it to the next level. Mr. Sanborn believes that by improving ourselves one day at a time and by competing with ourselves instead of others, we can all become extraordinary people living extraordinary lives.

Fred is great but Fred has limits

What I had found however, was that during drawn out periods of struggle, there are bounds beyond which being an extraordinary person doesn't guarantee the self-satisfaction it should. The limitation I found with the Fred Factor was that it no longer seemed to fit my own personal circumstances or those of the team I worked so closely with. By all reasonable standards we were Fred-like. For me personally and for most of life, I found this to be an enriching and deeply satisfying experience but now I was struggling as were those around me.

We had been working in an extremely challenging and uncertain situation and it had been this way for more than nine months with absolutely no letting up. On top of this, the company's finances were not the healthiest and we had this weighing on us as well. We needed to find a way to augment the principles of exceling to account for these types of circumstances. Everybody wants to feel satisfaction from the work they do, especially when they're giving all they have to give. Couldn't there be a few principles that if lived by, would guarantee self-satisfaction for any person striving to be extraordinary, no matter what the circumstances; even when an exciting challenge becomes at risk of degenerating into what can seem to be a never ending, high stress situation?

The challenge I found with applying the Fred Factor was that I didn't know how to account for this type of situation. The examples in the book were of a housekeeping supervisor, a flight attendant, a bartender, and of course; a postman. Although I'm sure all these professions have their own pressures, it seemed to me that most people involved in this type of work could probably go home after a hard day at work and relax; taking their mind off the pressures until they return to work the next day. Would a bad day or an unfortunate mistake lead to other people, good people, losing their job? Would a bad decision have the potential to do devastating harm to the company or even end its existence? Possibly: but probably not. However a lot of professionals do deal with these kinds of pressure every day. To be successful and to feel successful can be separate realities. To be successful we must consistently add value, rise above the expectations of others and work well with our co-workers. By succeeding at these activities we become essential to the company we work for. To feel successful however, we must create and maintain an enriching experience in our lives and work, through all situations both good and bad.

We shouldn't accept one without the other and need to consistently strive for both. There has to be a way to detach from the pressure without detaching from the commitment; to go beyond the status quo without sacrificing our health or happiness; to care deeply about succeeding yet not allow that care to be the mask hiding an underlying stress. Succeeding at this allows us to become extraordinary people truly leading extraordinary lives.

Chapter 3

Not all Jobs are the Same (Pressure Effect)

Not all professions are equal when it comes to day to day pressure and responsibility. A postman has his daily pressures I'm sure; traffic, unfriendly dogs, irritable customers and delivering on time; but consider the pressures that some must endure for prolonged periods:

Consider the owner of small business who's not getting the revenue needed to make ends meet. Not only is his or her livelihood and dream in danger, but there's also the added pressure that good people might have to be let go. It's one thing to let underperformers go; that can be difficult sometimes but it's clear the root cause rests with the individual. It's in each of our own power to make ourselves a valuable asset to the company were working for and if we're not living up to a high enough standard then changes can be expected. That being said, it's a different situation when we have excellent individuals on our team but find ourselves in a situation where we can no longer sustain them. Where does the responsibility lie in this case; especially for the owner who is ultimately responsible for the making the company a success?

Or what about the leader of a multi-million dollar, first of a kind technology project in a small start-up company.   Seemingly unlimited technical challenges coupled with limited funds and time; new and unknown challenges lurking behind every corner and countering every small success; readily knowing that your personal failure could result in the failure of the entire the company and wreak havoc on your own life as well as your friends and coworkers.

Or those careers where life and death literally hang in the balance every day: a surgeon committed to saving lives that eventually must end or a military person fighting for the better good. In either case a personal failure could result in the death or injury of innocent people who are counting on them with their lives.

Another example is those of us who find ourselves in the wrong career or working for the wrong company; stuck in a situation that's unsatisfying and wholly unfulfilling. It might not be our job on the line or the lives of those around us, but instead it's our dreams that are threatened as we risk not living up to our own priorities or standards of success.

Tolerance to pressure

All of us have our own tolerance to pressure. As long as we stay within our tolerance range, we can perform well, excel in our work, and maintain our happiness and health. If we allow ourselves to be pushed outside of our range however, pressure begins to transform into stress. One of our primary goals needs to be to expand our tolerance to pressure or if possible, to remove it altogether.

Pressure does not have to equal stress, although sometimes it's hard to separate the two. Pressure is a measure of the level of challenge we face; an acknowledgement of what's at stake; what's on the line. Stress on the other hand, is a measure of our physiological response to that pressure; the level of effect the pressure has on our physical and mental well-being. Being in high pressure situations can cause some people to thrive and others to shutdown depending on that person's individual tolerance range. Even those who thrive however, will eventually burn out if the exposure is too great or too long.

To succeed in these types of situations requires us to consciously and purposefully increase our own tolerance to pressure and to help others who might also be struggling. Increasing our tolerance range allows us to continue to excel at what we do while feeling good about ourselves and our efforts in the process. Increasing our tolerance to pressure allows extraordinary people to remain extraordinary even in exceptional circumstances. A great deal of this book will focus on how we can increase our tolerance to pressure both proactively as well as in unexpected situations.

Chapter 4

All jobs are the Same (Insecurity Effect)

Whether you love or hate your job; whether you're good at it, great at it, or an underachiever; you will most likely, one day lose your job. The only question is when. Forgive me if I sound pessimistic; I'm not. This isn't the same world our grandparents or parents grew up in. Companies downsize, get acquired, and fail every day and every time that happens some of us will need to move on. As professionals we can either ignore the signs of the times, live in fear of the inevitable, or accept it as fact and prepare accordingly.

Fred worked for the United States Postal Service. The U.S. postal service is one of the largest money losing organizations in the world. One day Fred will probably lose his job. It's almost a certainty. The mail business simply can't survive as it did fifty years ago. The fact that we perform our work with passion and high standards will have little effect on the corporate decision to downsize when the time comes.

Passionate workers who excel in their work might be spared for a time, but especially in careers where employees work independently and with little oversight or notice from their top management, even exceptional employees may find themselves out of work as a part of what might seem to be random acts of cost cutting or because the company just can't make ends meet. Companies like Enron or Leman Brother's go from being global powerhouses one day to being maimed or not existing at all the next. Thousands of hard working, talented people have woken up to realize that despite the fact they gave it their all, despite the fact they exceled at what they did, they were just as out of work as the next person.

In today's environment we have to take responsibility for our lives. Companies fail every day and it's not for the lack of trying. Competition is fierce and the very nature of competition assumes there will be some winners and some losers.

Lack of job security doesn't have to equal stress. This may seem easier said than done. I have a personal experience in which I was put under a huge amount of stress because of fearing for my job. I came to work one day to find out we had lost a major project; one that I was heavily involved in. This particular project had supported about one third of the company and everyone knew we had a big problem on our hands. To make matters worse, I had just purchased my first house two months earlier. Mine was the sole income of a family with two toddlers, in a city we had only recently moved to and knew practically no one. For my family, life was just starting out and the risk of losing my job now was terrifying to me. I recall vividly that my stress was very real to me and very visible to those around me. It took about two months before the layoffs came and waiting through that period was agonizing. All I can say is I was one of the lucky ones but thirty-three of my coworkers weren't. There was a mix of reactions from the group that was let go; some cried; some were angry; some were noticeably anxious; but a few seemed surprisingly calm. I later found out that at least one of the calm ones already had another job lined up. He had been actively looking from the day we lost the project two months earlier. While most of us were anxiously sitting around waiting to see what was going to happen, this person was proactively setting up a contingency plan. He didn't know for certain he would need one but he knew he might, and by doing so was able to comfortably face a very uncomfortable situation.

As you navigate through the remaining sections of this book you'll see that the overall message is simple. Be extraordinary, but do it for you rather than needing some kind reward or acknowledgment from others. Be extraordinary, no matter what the circumstances and no matter what the pressure. Hopefully the tools outlined here will allow you to do just that; they've certainly made a big impact on my life and on my career.

Part 2

How to Be Extraordinary

* Chapter 5 *

Bringing Out the Best in Others – People Skills

<u>Treat people decently</u>

Pay attention to what others do. Notice what their working on and whether or not their having a good day. We all want to be appreciated and feel as though our work is important and paying some simple notice to others can do just that. When we see somebody in the break room or have a short hallway conversation, we can say something like, "I saw you working on <u>*fill in blank*</u>, it looks like it's really coming along." It doesn't need to be anything more involved than that, just enough to show we notice the work others do and acknowledge it. This small amount of effort gives others a boost and builds subtle bonds that strengthen relationships.

Invest some energy to meet the people you work with. We don't need to be overly social but we should take a minute to introduce ourselves and give a polite smile and accompanying hello when we walk by someone in the halls. A simple hello to people we don't work directly with or frequently with, builds respect and bonds. To make it really meaningful use their name when you say hello. We respond better when someone addresses us by our name and by doing so, we'll be building alliances throughout the company. One approach is to take five minutes once a week or so and walk around the building casually looking for people you don't know. If you find someone, give a quick hello and introduce yourself, then move on. After that, it's a simple hello as they're walking by.

Be interested in the opinions of others. When there are opinions to be heard, listen to them. Actively seek them out. Often, we hone in on a solution too quickly and our decision is based only on our own limited background and experience. Others in the organization, with different skills and backgrounds will have their own views and opinions that can be very different from our own. Listening to the perspective of others and the reasoning behind their opinions can give new information that helps us make the best decision. Sometimes there's more than one solution to a problem. When this is the case we should be comfortable with our solution not being the one selected. This is especially true if we're not the ones doing the actual work. Letting the people responsible for getting the job done choose the manner in which they'll do the work can empower them to do it right. It shows we have faith in them and respect their competence.

Give respect as your default position. We have a choice; we can either take the position that people must earn our respect before we give it or we can openly give respect and make people lose it before we take it away. By choosing the latter we build solid relationships with far more people than we would otherwise. Respect and trust are two way streets for most of us; if someone treats us with respect and trust, we're more apt to treat them the same way. We recognize and respond to the respect we receive from others. Would we rather give our best to someone who lacks basic respect and trust for us or our work, or would we rather go all out for someone who thinks highly of us and believes we can get the job done right?

Give opportunity. Just as we don't want to get stuck in a dead end job, neither does anybody else. By giving people new opportunities we give them a chance to grow and expand their skills and field of influence. Most of us respond positively to new challenges and our respect grows for those who give us new opportunities. It's a way of confirming that we recognize not only the value the person is providing today, but also the potential they have within. As we give opportunities however, we should make sure we're not setting someone up for failure. Opportunities should be given safely at first to provide "safe experiments" where it's ok to fail. It allows us to develop others without risking a bad outcome for them or us. As capabilities develop, the opportunities will naturally become higher profile. We should never fear other's success. On the contrary, we should develop those around us to the best extent possible. Being surrounded by extraordinary people helps us become extraordinary. Like begets like; greatness begets greatness.

Stand up for your team. None of us are perfect and mistakes happen; sometimes high profile mistakes. We should always be on the lookout for ways to improve and be willing to admit when things haven't gone according to plan, but we should never let our teammates become the target of blame. Except in situations where we are recommending ending a working relationship with someone, our focus should be on presenting solutions to problems rather than assigning blame for mistakes. Sometimes people are looking for someone to blame for a situation. Our goal is to redirect what otherwise could become a dangerous conversation into one that focuses on finding a path for moving forward and achieving success. In parallel, and especially if the mistake could have been avoided, we should work with the person to make sure they learn from the experience.

Be honest with yourself and others

Being honest builds trust even if the message isn't a positive one. Most of us want to be told the truth instead of being told everything's fine when we already know it's not. We quickly lose trust and respect for those who don't have the courage to face the truth of the situation. It's almost human nature to try and make things seem not as bad as they really are. Taken to the extreme, this results in closing our eyes to the problems we face instead of courageously facing them. It wouldn't be the first time a company failed because there was a problem lurking under the surface that nobody had the courage to face. When things are good; say so. When things are bad; say so. Being honest with ourselves and others is the first step in overcoming any challenge.

Don't shy away from difficult conversations. Although difficult conversations can be uncomfortable for everyone involved, they are an important part of being able to bring out the best in others. Difficult conversations are meant to improve the situation for everyone and if done properly, can build trust and respect between parties. Being honest with others is the first step to building a world class team.

<u>Give praise sparingly; give thanks frequently.</u>

Honest appreciation will bring out the best in others and reinforce their belief that they're playing an important role and contributing to the success of the company. The way in which we show appreciation is to give genuine thanks to people for their effort. Keep it real and when possible, thank them in person instead of doing it by email.

Use praise sparingly and only in exceptional circumstances. Thanks tells someone we appreciate their effort, their workmanship, their attention to detail, etc. Praise says we believe they went above and beyond their capabilities, our expectations, or have done something exceptional. We should have high standards for ourselves and for those around us and shouldn't expect praise for doing our job nor give to freely when others do theirs. Giving or receiving a sincere thank-you on the other hand, tells us our work is important and is being noticed.

Take responsibility and give credit when it's due

Taking responsibility when things aren't going as planned is a sign of character and courage. If we are to be extraordinary we can't hide from our problems or be timid about speaking up to say we could've done a better job. It takes courage to face our mistakes and admit them to others but it's the act of doing so that allows us to grow and improve for the future.   The same is true when we accomplish what we set out to do. Not only do we take the responsibility that is rightfully ours, but we also give credit where credit is due. When things go right, we make it heard who the individuals were that helped pull it all together. We don't give credit just to those at the top of the chain either. Although it's often true that those at the top give us strategy and guide us towards a successful outcome, it's more true that those actually performing the work are the ones going the extra mile to make it all work. Vocally and consistently giving credit to those who deserve it builds a sense of team and mutual respect and beyond that, it's the right thing to do.

Have a collaborative spirit but know when to call it off and be assertive

Many career coaches will discuss the advantages of collaboration in problem solving and resolving conflicts.

The reasoning often used is that it builds team spirit and can result in both parties achieving their goals and coming out on top. Although this is true, it's not the primary benefit of using collaboration. When it comes to overcoming challenges, collaboration can often, although not always, lead to a better solution than if we were to go it alone. This is the primary purpose for collaborating with others: to come up with the best possible solution to a problem. By including others in the discussion and listening to their perspectives and reasoning, we often find that what we had thought was the best solution really wasn't. Collaboration is used as an effective tool in decision making because it helps make sure we've sought out all the information available before making an important decision. If it builds teams and helps a group of individuals feel they contributed to the solution, then this is an added benefit but not the primary purpose. Use collaboration as a tool to pick the best solution from all the possible choices we have before us.

There comes a time in the collaboration process when a final decision must be made. At this point it's about making the best decision and not at all about building teams or making sure each party is satisfied with the outcome. In the long run, we'll be most respected for making good decisions, not for making sure everybody's satisfied. The best pathway for making good decisions however, is to seek perspectives and ideas from others. Even if an individual is not satisfied with the outcome, he or she will appreciate the respect given them by having their opinions considered. In most cases, those of us who initiate the collaboration process will find our own solution isn't the one we ultimately choose. This is a sign that collaboration works. In all cases, appreciation should be given to everyone involved in the process so they understand the importance of their input.

Chapter 6

Bringing Out the Best in Ourselves – Personal Skills

<u>Project quiet confidence</u>

Have you ever met someone who effortlessly exudes confidence; someone whose confidence is obvious just by looking at him? I'm not referring to voiced confidence; statements like "we can do this" or "we're going to succeed", but rather to unspoken confidence; the kind that lifts your spirit just by being around them. Quiet confidence is a trait we should all develop and can do so by following a few basic principles.

Be at ease with yourself. We all have strengths; we all have weaknesses. Quietly confident people know themselves enough to recognize their strengths and weaknesses. They know they have flaws but accept them and aren't ashamed of them. They don't try to change who they are depending on the situation. It doesn't matter if they're talking to the mailroom clerk, an underperforming employee, or the CEO of the company; they consistently project their real self.

You can tell a quietly confident person by the way they sit, the way they walk, and by the way look at you. Quietly confident people are relaxed but not lazy. They sit relaxed but with good posture; not slouching nor stiff. They walk with purpose; not rushed; not wandering. They look at you honestly no matter the situation. Their eyes don't pierce nor are they unfocused with lack of caring or interest.

Quietly confident people don't boast and aren't arrogant. Being arrogant or boasting of our success is a sign we need acceptance from others; that we're somehow looking for someone's approval or that we have to prove something to those around us. Quietly confident people prove to themselves instead of to others and by doing so, silently project their success. There is a natural genuineness encompassing them that's felt by those around them.

Being quietly confident calms those around us. Being at ease with ourselves naturally puts us at ease with others and allows others to be at ease with us. To become quietly confident we develop our awareness and strive to see ourselves as others see us.

Convey believable optimism

We all want to be optimistic about the future and for those around us to share in our optimism. Nothing is worse however than someone telling us that everything's going to be ok when we know it's not. Optimism is only credible, if it's believable and by pushing unbelievable optimism, we risk losing our credibility all together. Believable optimism is authentic; unbelievable optimism is at best naïve and at worst dishonest. To bring out the best in ourselves and in those around us, we need to consistently convey believable optimism.

Believable optimism doesn't imply that we're trying to make people feel good about a bad situation. It implies we're going to get through the situation. In order to convey this message we need to be realistic about what we're up against. We need to recognize the challenges we face and be open about them instead of trying to hide them from others. Believable optimism comes with a stark honest evaluation of the situation followed by forging a plan to maneuver through the maze of problems ahead of us.   Optimism isn't about ignoring our problems and hoping they'll go away. It's about accepting the reality of the situation and figuring out a way to overcome the obstacles.

Having believable optimism ourselves is good, but conveying it to those around us is better. To convey believable optimism we need to be open about the challenges that lie ahead as well as the solutions that will allow us to prevail. By projecting honesty about a situation and having a commitment to finding a solution, we build trust and enable others to form the resolve needed to achieve success. Believable optimism opens the door to building a sense of ownership throughout the team; a sense of personal commitment to do what needs to be done in order to succeed.

Maintain a calm focus

In order to focus on anything we have to know what it is we're after. We have to understand what the end point is; what the goal is we're trying to achieve. This should be explicit, not implied. There should be no doubt from us or those around us as to what it is were working towards. Understanding the end state defines success, or rather shows us what success looks like. If you're on a team, it's vitally important that every member understands what the ultimate goal is they're going after. Otherwise it's almost certain we'll stray from the path of success and wander dangerously off course.

Extraordinary people make it a point to know the true goal and to take deliberate and continuous actions toward that goal; not allowing distractions to veer them in a different direction; recognizing when obstacles arise and then skillfully maneuvering around them with minimum disruption to their journey.

It's common for some to become lost in the details of their work; to confuse a curiosity with the actual goal they're seeking. This is ordinary; not extraordinary. If an action isn't moving us closer to the ultimate goal; if it doesn't help us form the picture of success that we've laid out before us, then it shouldn't be done. Time and energy are being wasted instead of harnessed.

Similarly we should expect to be surprised along the way. An onslaught of challenges lies between mediocrity and greatness. When something unexpected happens, it interferes with our strategy; it interferes with our timing. The extraordinary ones among us aren't shaken and don't lose sight of the end state or become engulfed within the challenge. Challenges are just obstacles and obstacles are just realities we must deal with along the way. Our only focus on obstacles is in finding a way to maneuver around them in order to get back on the path to our destination.

To be truly extraordinary, to be among the elite, not only do we remain focused on the end point but we do so with great calmness; calmness even when under fire from a barrage of unexpected challenges. Our calmness becomes the anchor for those around us to attach to. Our focus becomes the light illuminating the path forward.

There are many leaders who cannot lead and there are many followers who lead silently from within. No matter what position we hold, by maintaining calm focus we gracefully and steadfastly guide ourselves and our team in the direction of success.

Manage your mood

We all have bad days and sometimes it doesn't take much to push us over the edge. To be the best we can be, we have to be able to manage our emotions. We've all experienced the uplifting feeling we get when we're around other happy people or the emotional drag when we're around sad or depressed ones. The most extraordinary of us understand this effect and take advantage of it to brighten our own mood as well as those around us. The most important time to smile is when we don't want to and a good laugh can lift anybody's spirits. We should get into the habit of being friendly to others and smiling when we interact with them. This requires a commitment to letting go of the emotional traps so many of us fall into.

Don't confuse this with pretending to be happy when you're not. Happiness begets happiness and sadness begets sadness. Sometimes someone has to jump start the process. If we commit to creating the spark that ignites the spirits of those around us, then their rise will in turn lift our spirits higher and continue fanning the flames which then further supports us both.

The opposite is also true and we must commit to not letting others bring us down nor allow ourselves to have a negative influence on others. Although most people are genuinely happy and want to keep it that way, some aren't and sometimes the best thing we can do is put on a little smile and walk away.

<u>Enjoy your work</u>

Most of us spend the majority of our time either at work or thinking about the work we need to do. We owe it to ourselves to get some level of enjoyment and satisfaction from something that's going to take such a large percentage of our time. Although getting a paycheck and making ends meet is essential to survival, we're kidding ourselves if our own suffering is the price we're willing to pay. If we're not satisfied with our career then it's up to us to get it on track. We can do this by looking for opportunities and developing the skills necessary to move us in the right direction. This will be covered in much more detail in section four - Make yourself in-demand.

* Chapter 7 *

Delivering the Goods – Professional Skills

<u>Be in the now; look to the past; drive to the future</u>

Focusing on the destination is vital but so is knowing exactly where we are along the way and exactly where we're coming from. As we take on more and more responsibilities this skill becomes essential. It takes a great amount of planning, awareness, and wisdom to bring together all the elements with just the right timing that make up a complex project or task.

1. Be in the now

Our ability to be aware of what's going on at any giving time, combined with the ability to effectively deal with the barrage of day to day problems and issues as they occur, is what separates those who are masters of execution from those who struggle. We need to develop awareness, not in the general sense but specifically for the critical aspects that can either keep things moving forward or send them spiraling off course. A keen eye for identify missing elements and a knack for solving problems in real time are two important skills we should consciously develop. A good way to start developing this is to start doing it.

At the beginning of each week, spend an hour or so going over the major items that need accomplished over the next seven days. Write them down in a list that you can check off one by one. Spend some time asking yourself simple questions like; Are the right tools and people in place to do the work? Have we forgotten anything? What can go wrong? Then at the start of each day thereafter, spend 15-20 minutes following up on whether or not things are going as planned. If a problem has come up, plan accordingly on how to solve it. If everything's going smoothly then spend a few minutes thinking about what's going to be happening next.

2. Look to the past

Don't get trapped in a cycle of repeating mistakes. Realize that if we're to learn from our mistakes, we must first recognize them. The three types of mistakes that can haunt us are poor planning, poor execution, and poor decision making.

Poor planning includes things like setting unrealistic timelines, not including critical items, or failing to recognize interconnections between steps. Our plan is our map to get us to the destination we desire and without a good map we're sure to get lost. If we assume we'll cross the mountain in a week and packed rations accordingly, what will we do if the trip ends ups taking a month: will we survive? If our map leads us to an impassible chasm; then what? Take time to plan smart and review that plan frequently.

Poor execution includes things like not giving enough attention to notice when things are going off track or becoming too slack when we believe things are going well instead of maintaining a constant push forward. Getting ahead of the game and then staying ahead are the keys to winning. How many of us have watched our favorite sports team get a comfortable lead and then get lazy and ultimately lose? A winning execution strategy includes a consistent and relentless push towards the finish line no matter whether or not we believe we're temporarily ahead of, or behind our original expectations.

Poor decision making is often the result of not focusing on the desired end state or from fighting the wrong battle. Each of our decisions should be taking us towards the final goal. If it's not, then it might be a poor one. It does no good to fight valiantly and capture one hill when strategically, it was a different one needed to win the war. Many of us get lost in day to day problems and issues, and sometimes make decisions we believe are good at the time but which don't advance us towards the ultimate goal, or worse, take us in the wrong direction.

We will make mistakes and if we look close enough, we'll almost always see we could have done things better. What separates the extraordinary from the ordinary is the ability to learn from those mistakes and not repeat them.

3. Drive to the future

To drive to the future requires that we first scan the horizon to see what lies ahead of us. When there is uncharted territory, we send out scouts to identify the risks and then act accordingly. We can make it a lot easier on ourselves if we recognize and solve problems before they become a crisis. This makes the difference between what would seem to be an almost effortless execution of a project and one that's riddled in urgency. Our winning strategy includes developing the ability to look out in front of where we are, identify potential stumbling blocks, and remove them long before anyone else recognizes them to be problem. This can range from simple things like making sure everything's set up a ready to go ahead of time, to recognizing areas where something new is planned and then making sure there's nothing new about it by the time it's actually needed.

Say what you do; do what you say; have it done when you said it would be

A common philosophy in business is to "say what we do and do what we say". The idea behind this is to be transparent with others about what we're signing up for and be willing to be held accountable for completing it. Taking it a step further, we want to be clear and open about telling others when we'll be finished by and willing to be held accountable for meeting the timeline we've laid out. It's by combining these principles that we raise ourselves beyond average performance to extraordinary performance.

Many times we focus only on the items we consider most important. When we do this we risk letting some of the smaller ones slip through the cracks. It's natural to prioritize what needs to get done and focus on the highest priority items first. The problem that comes up is that the ones lower down on the priority list stay there and often keep getting pushed back by others things we consider to be more important.

Other times we're bombarded with little things that just aren't that important. They're always brought with a sense of urgency however, and if we're not careful we can get lost in the confusion and neglect the things we should be focusing the majority of our efforts on.

Say what we do; do what we say; and have it done when we said it would be. To be successful we need to be selective about what we sign up to do. Don't take on commitments that you can't keep. When we do this, we're setting ourselves up for failure. If we commit to completing something, it's not ok to come back later and say "I didn't get to it because of this or that". If that's the case, we shouldn't have said we'd get it done in the first place. Being extraordinary means taking your commitments seriously and completing them. We need to keep in mind that what's small to us might be big to someone else. If we agree to complete something by a certain date we've essentially given our word to do so. If we don't deliver on what we've committed to, then we're making a statement about how we value the promises we make.

If we believe something isn't worth doing or if we can't commit the time it takes to do it right, then we shouldn't sign up for it. Don't be timid about saying no when somebody asks you to do something you can't deliver on and don't be timid about not signing up to a timeline that you won't be able to keep. Not only do we need to be clear about what we are signing up for, we also need to be clear about what we're not signing up for.

Sometimes we get asked to do things we don't know how to complete. That's ok. If you don't know how to do it, your role is to find somebody who does; not just let it sit. Sometimes we get asked to do things we don't like doing. That's ok too. If you don't like to do it, either do it anyway and get it over with or find somebody who enjoys that type of work.

For things that take longer; make steady progress. As little as 15-30 minutes a day spent on loose ends will keep you from stalling out down the road. We've all heard Thomas Jefferson's quote, "Don't put off till tomorrow what you can get done today". To be extraordinary we need to take it to the next level and say "Don't put off until later what we can do right now". Knock the quick things off the list as soon as they come. If information needs to be passed along so others can do what they need to do, then by all means don't hold onto it; get it out there so things can keep moving.

Say what we do; do what we say; have it done when we said it would be. Don't just treat this as simple saying. Make this an integral part of your performance and you'll excel well beyond those around you.

Part 3

How to Be Extraordinary

Under Pressure

Chapter 8

When Things Turn Bad

In order to become extraordinary under pressure, we must first be able recognize the difference between pressure and stress. There's a fine line between the two and they are often confused. Stress is a physiological response to pressure but it's not the pressure itself. Pressure sets the level of urgency, the level of importance, the level of visibility. Understanding what's at stake allows us to better prepare and do what needs to be done. Stress on the other hand, is a response to a threatening situation. Although stress can be helpful in an emergency, there reaches a point where it causes damage to our health, our mood, our productivity, and our relationships. Prolonged exposure to stress can literally destroy our quality of life. Consider these differences between being under pressure and being under stress:

- Pressure can be a powerful motivator whereas stress can leave us uncaring.

- Pressure can bring out the best in us whereas stress can bring out the worst.

- Pressure can raise us to a higher level of performance whereas stress can shut us down almost completely.

To avoid letting pressure transform into stress, we'll have to learn to separate our emotions from the pressure we're under. To do this we'll have to learn to detach, let go, and become neutral to the pressures we face without allowing ourselves to detach, let go, or become neutral to the job we've committed ourselves to do. This means we'll have to learn to control our physiological response so that it doesn't affect our ability to make good decisions or our ability to execute efficiently. We'll need to become more aware of our response to pressure and by doing so, learn to recognize the first signs of when pressure is transforming into stress. Then we'll proactively take charge and stop the transformation all together.

Recognize when stress starts build

We need to recognize when stress is starting to affect us and those around us and then stop it before it gets out of control. Sometimes the signs are obvious. I once had a difficult conversation with someone who was under extreme stress and he had a strong physiological response. At first his lip quivered as he spoke, then his eye started to twitch. I knew he was in a difficult situation and I was trying to help him find a solution. Just being in the position of talking about it however, was pushing him over the edge and I become nothing less than shocked when a stream of blood began to run steadily from his nose.

When we're working under stress our usual coping mechanism is to try to suppress it instead of dissolve it. This is not a good approach. We can only suppress stress for a limited time before something comes along and ignites a reaction. For example, if we're experiencing stress because we have too much to get done and not enough time to do it, then we might have a strong reaction to someone who comes along and asks us to do something else, or inadvertently gets in the way of us doing our work. If we've been suppressing our stress, a simple situation like this can provoke a disproportionate response and we might say or do something we'll regret later by acting less professional than we should.

Common emotional signs of stress include moodiness, irritability, a sense of being overwhelmed, depression, or feeling alone. We can also have a physical reaction and feel exhausted, overly anxious, or even get sick more often. When under these kinds of conditions we're more prone to make poor decisions, procrastinate, or even lose our ability to function at work.

We have to learn to recognize the first signs of stress in ourselves and others and then proactively diffuse it. It's far easier to diffuse stress at its onset than after its gotten out of control. Even beyond that, we can follow some simple guidelines to keep stress from growing in the first place. We owe it to ourselves to maintain our health and happiness as well as keep our composure and professionalism.

Chapter 9

Know Your Priorities

<u>What are your real priorities?</u>

Each of us is different; we have our own set of values, our own personal dreams to fulfill, and our own sense of what's important to us. It's not anybody's place to tell someone else what their priorities are or should be. This is for us to decide alone. It's our responsibility to recognize what's important to us and make sure the way we spend our time and the decisions we make move us in the right direction.

Priorities can be broken down different ways. We can talk about life priorities, career priorities, long term priorities, and short term priorities. Whatever they are however, they are ours to decide as only we are capable of doing. It's important for us to know our real priorities and make a commitment not to lose sight of them in the day to day craziness of life.

The routine of everyday life is a powerful obscurer of our real priorities. A fear of death on the other hand, is a powerful reminder of them. We can't, or at least shouldn't, wait until we're facing the eternal before realizing we've missed the opportunity to accomplish those things that are most deeply important to us.

It's easy to confuse our short term priorities with our long term ones or to focus exclusively on career priorities and forget about our life ones. To keep this from happening we should take an hour or so and write them down. By doing this we clear our mind from uncertainty and can better focus our decisions on achieving what's most important to us. We should make a determined commitment to be true to ourselves and let our priorities guide us. Living consistent with what's most important to us helps ensure our happiness and the level of fulfillment we get out of life. No matter how strong our determination and persistence is, we can't succeed at this unless we know what our real priorities are. Too many of us are so caught up in our daily responsibilities we only realize those things most important to us after we lose them and sometimes we develop an enormous emotional attachment to something that in the grand scheme of things, is utterly meaningless.

One way to determine our priorities is to imagine ourselves later in life, reflecting back. We want to be in a position where our regrets are kept to an absolute minimum and to feel satisfied with the life we've lived. We're all different; there's no right or wrong priorities. Take some time and write them down. As a point of reference, here's a list of my own.

Short Term Life Priorities:

1. I want to be part an integral part of my children's lives as they grow up. I want to be there to see it and be part of the experience; not just hear stories afterwards.

2. I want to spend quality time with my wife and not let the day to day craziness of life and work keep that from happening.

3. I want to have and maintain a financial plan that's plausible. One that will allow me to retire at a reasonable age.

4. I want to stay healthy and active and take regular walks so I can experience a world not bounded by four walls.

Short Term Career Priorities

1. I want to enjoy my career and feel like I make a difference in what I do. I want my work to mean something to me and the company I work for.

2. I want to be respected; not blindly, but because I excel at what I do.

3. I want to put my career on my own personal path to success. I want to be able to start my own company. I want to recognize and take every opportunity that can help me achieve this.

4. I want to stay true to those around me and give credit where it's due, give opportunity to others, and maintain a collaborative spirit.

Long Term Life Priorities

1. I want to have the kind of relationship with my children where we're not be afraid to say "I love you"

when they're grown and I'm old. I want us to have a strong mutual respect for each other, our lives, and even for the decisions they make that I might not agree with. I want them to miss me when I pass and to have many fond memories to choose from to remember me by.

2. I want to continually grow closer to my wife instead of growing apart as so many couples do. I want us to depend on each other and for our love to stay strong through whatever happens as we move forward in our lives. I want us to walk hand in hand when we're old and talk, listen, and understand what's really important to each other.

3. I want to live comfortably as a senior, not necessarily extravagantly. I want to have a nice home and be able to do some traveling with my wife without having to worry about how we're going to pay our bills.

4. I want of be proud of the things I do and the decisions I make. I don't want to put myself in a position of reflecting back on my life saying "I wish I hadn't done

_____" or "I wish I had done _____". I want to stand up for what I believe in even if it means taking a risk and realize that the larger risk is to compromise my long term values for a short term relief of not having to face my fear.

Long Term Career Priorities

1. I want to start my own business that at least maintains my current standard of living.

Use your priorities to manage stress

Once we know our real priorities, we can leverage them to manage the pressures we face so that our stress remains at a minimum. Not only does keeping a close eye on our priorities help manage stress, it also helps make sure we achieve what's most important to us. When we're working in high pressure situations, an occasional reminder of our most personal goals helps us realize how small our current situation is in comparison. Keeping this fresh in our mind allows us to face high pressure situations through a lens focused on what's most important rather than letting temporary circumstances take over and the associated stress take hold.

Keep Things in Perspective

<u>Don't transform an unexpected event into a crisis</u>

When we're caught up in the moment, an unexpected event can sometimes seem larger and more important than it actually is. Unexpected situations add pressure to our work by posing a threat to the timeline we've laid out and by adding uncertainty to what our results will be. Any threat can induce stress and especially in the initial stages of an unexpected situation, when we're sorting through the unknowns and uncertainties surrounding the event, we're at risk to experience a physical reaction. We need to accept that surprises will occur and prepare ourselves to the best extent as we can to accommodate the inconvenience without letting it affect us mentally or physically.

The vast majority of setbacks we'll face are going to be minor and as long as we handle them expediently and efficiently, coupled with a professional attitude, they'll pose little risk or threat for things not working out. Understanding this will reduce the ability of a surprise situation to impact our level of stress. There's a common saying, "Don't sweat the small stuff" that we should make a point to live by. For smaller inconveniences:

- We should expect them and not allow them to frustrate us

- We should deal with them quickly and decisively and get back on track as soon as possible

On the occasion when something big gets in our way, treat it as challenge rather than a threat. Not all setbacks are minor and some might present real challenges to overcome. In these situations we need to be prepared to execute a pre-determined strategy designed to remove the obstacles and get us back on the right path. The more prepared we are beforehand, the less likely we'll subject ourselves to unhealthy levels of stress. Although it's not practical to have a detailed plan in place for a surprise before it occurs, it is possible to have a generic plan of action we can implement if needed.   For more major setbacks our default plan should be:

- Gather as much information as possible

- Get the right people involved

- Create a plan of attack

- Execute

- Review the status and adjust as necessary

By having a basic strategy for handling setbacks, we're better able to maintain our perspective on the situation. Our focus should never be on us but should always be on the situation. We should never feel threatened, only challenged to succeed. By being ready to implement a strategy as soon as a situation unfolds allows us to face the challenge with confidence. Having confidence supports having a healthy perspective which in turn keeps our stress low even when the pressure is high.

Learn to step back from the situation and refocus

The healthiest perspective we can have is one that allows us to look forward to each day. Drudging coming to work day after day is a sign that something needs to change and often, what needs to change is our perspective towards our life and our work. When we find ourselves struggling with our happiness and wellbeing, it's time to remember what our real priorities are and reevaluate our progress towards achieving them.

Sometimes the best thing we can do is to step outside ourselves for a moment and view the landscape around us from a different set of eyes. This includes viewing ourselves, our attitude, and our effectiveness at dealing with the circumstances surrounding us. When things aren't going well, sometimes it's fruitful to imagine we've just been brought into the situation for the first time and asked to solve it. If someone were to come in new to the situation they would have the advantage of a fresh perspective that isn't colored by the events or pressures of the past. Occasionally we need to reset our perspective and try to recapture this within ourselves. If we were starting a new job, at a different company and the first item we were asked to tackle was this high pressure, perhaps struggling project, how would our attitude and perspective be different than it is now? Would our strategy be different? Would our measure of success be the same? Would our confidence level be altered from what it is today? Learn to step outside yourself from time to time in order to force a different perspective and you'll put yourself in a stronger position to avoid letting the pressures of your day to day life transform into stress.

Chapter 11

Become a Cold Blooded Professional

<u>Be neutral to the pressure but not to the people or the result you're after</u>

There's a difference between being neutral and being numb. Neutrality doesn't imply lack of caring or lack of commitment whereas numbness could be construed that way. Being neutral implies that no matter what happens we're going to make sure we have the state of mind needed to be at our best and to succeed at what we do.

In order to succeed we maintain the healthy relationships and work strategies that allow us to stand out from the crowd, no matter what the stakes are we're playing for. Neutrality is a frame of mind that has little to do with the circumstances going on around us. Being neutral requires an awareness about how we're handling a situation from the inside as well as how we're executing a strategy externally. Being aware of our internal state allows us to make adjustments to our perspective at the slightest sign of stress. To adjust our perspective we use the tools outlined earlier: we step back from the situation and view it from a different perspective and while doing so, we remind ourselves of what our real priorities are and make sure were satisfying our needs.

To be extraordinary, we must be professionals; even more than that, we must strive to be high performing professionals. Professionalism implies being capable of keeping our emotions under control when the pressure is on. The pressure will be what it will, but as high performing professionals we're expected to deal with it and not let it come between us and achieving the result we were hired to attain. Achieving the desired end state, no matter what the pressures are, should always stay focused in our minds.

We're here for one reason: to get the job done.

We're hired to perform. If we don't or can't perform at the level expected, then we haven't delivered on our part of the bargain and should expect that action will be taken. Our state of mind has a huge influence on our ability to perform. We need to recognize this and set our mental state in an optimum way to sustain the highest levels of performance. This implies a certain level of emotional detachment about the means necessary to get to the end. It also implies that we maintain a persistent focus on the desired end state and take a professional attitude of not accepting that the goal won't be achieved.

Don't take anything personal

In professional boxing, two fighters battle with the sole purpose of inflicting pain and bodily damage on each other. Yet at the end of the match they shake hands and sometimes even give each other a hug. As professionals we need to have the same kind of attitude. We don't hold grudges against the people we work with and although we don't need to be the best of buddies, we should keep a professional demeanor and always maintain our composure.

If we receive criticism, constructive or otherwise, we deal with the issue and move on. There's a mix of personalities surrounding us and some of them can be uncomfortably direct. Maybe we excel at 95% of what we do but someone always seems to focus only on the 5% we're weak on. Don't dwell on it; don't take it personal; and don't hold it against the person. We're not so good that we can't improve and we shouldn't hold it against someone for pointing out those areas even if their communication skills are lacking. The worst thing we can do is get stuck in a state of denial and believe we're better than we actually are. To be extraordinary we recognize our weaknesses and work to improve them.

In the instances where criticism isn't constructive or factually based, calmly educate the person or group about the facts of the situation. Don't get upset or frustrated, just set the record straight. In the instances where others insult us or talk negatively behind our back, don't sweat it and definitely don't stoop to their level. People sometimes feel threatened by others success or their lack of it, and other times a person's frustration bubbles to the surface and they say things they don't really mean. Whatever the reason, our goal is to be extraordinary and we should have no part in it. We focus on treating people right and doing the best job we can possible do.

We should be comfortable knowing that nobody owes us anything and shouldn't try to convince ourselves otherwise. Don't rely on others' approval or recognition to validate your accomplishments. We validate ourselves by maintaining our real priorities, treating others with the respect they deserve and getting the job done right the first time. This doesn't imply we settle for working for those who aren't capable of giving appreciation when it's due, but we shouldn't hold it against them either. We just keep doing the best we're capable of and if it's not working out in our current position, then it's time to consider moving on to a better situation; no hard feelings, no animosity, just pure professionalism.

Chapter 12

Leading the Team

Lead by example

Emotional energy is contagious and we want to use it to our advantage. When a team is in a high stakes environment it's more important than ever to keep our perspective fresh and honest. We can't allow ourselves to be shaken by the challenges we face no matter how great. If we want to get the best out of others we have to give the best of ourselves and make it visible to those around us. When a team is working under pressure, a good role model can be essential and we should make a commitment to be that model. When team members see someone who's facing the same pressures they are, acting with calmness, focus and determination, it does more than just leave a positive impression; it develops an inner strength within them. By maintaining our composure, we set an extraordinary example that raises the bar of professionalism within the group.

Challenge gives meaning

Overcoming difficult challenges can make a good team great. It's what creates a world class organization and raises both individuals and teams to a level of excellence. To create and maintain an extraordinary team, we should aim to inspire members to view unexpected setbacks or other high pressure situations as challenges that by overcoming, set us apart from the ordinary or average person. In many ways the challenges we face, and the manner in which we respond to them, defines who we are and we mustn't forget that we get a say in who we want to be. Do we want to be continuously frustrated and under high amounts of stress or do we want to rise to the challenge and overcome the obstacles before us?

To support a team in achieving this level of excellence, sometimes we need to keep members from becoming too focused on the near term situation and more focused on the end state. We should remind the team of what success looks like and that if it were easy, anybody could do it. We need to let them know they have the skills and creativity necessary to overcome the challenges they face and accomplish something really special; something that not just anybody could do.

Finally, as challenges are met and overcome, we vocally give credit to the team. This is important in any situation, but even more so in a high pressure environment. This builds pride in the team and enhances their ability to stay focused in otherwise frustrating circumstances.

<u>Recognize burn out</u>

Know your people and be aware of their stress level. Some of us hide it better than others but if possible we should recognize when stress is building and dissolve it before it bubbles to surface. Different personalities show stress in different ways; some act frustrated or angry; others shut down and stop performing at the level their capable of; others show signs of anxiety or depression; and some get physically ill more often.

At the first signs of stress, one of your roles as a team leader is to talk them down from the ledge and help them get back on track. Sometimes a simple talk can do wonders to help someone vent a little steam. Sometimes people need to hear us say that's everything going to be ok. Sometimes people need an opportunity for some downtime to recharge their batteries and reset their attitude towards work.

The best ways to keep a team from burning out are the same ones we use to keep ourselves from burning out. Help them shift their perspective. Talk about their true priorities. Keep them focused on the end state. Fill them with believable optimism and lift their confidence by letting them know that no matter how bad the situation, the team has the skills, wisdom, and courage to work through it and come out on top.

Overcome resistance to change

Change can be uncomfortable. It has an element of the unknown that excites some but frightens many. Change can have many faces. Perhaps a project is coming to an end, the company is being restructured, or roles are being redefined. Often during a period of change we find ourselves in a situation where we're uncertain of what tomorrow will bring or feel that we'll need to prove ourselves all over again.

Change is inevitable. We should use this principle to set our attitudes and help others do so as well. We should view change as an opportunity, not an obstacle, and use it to drive us to a better place. We do this for ourselves and as leaders of a team we help others see it the same way. We should focus on the positive aspects of change but also realize that the transition itself can be uncomfortable. As extraordinary individuals we let our life goals guide us through periods of uncertainty while staying committed to achieving our priorities. If we can do this we'll come out winners at the end.

Chapter 13

If Things Get Really Bad

<u>Don't get mentally trapped by a temporary situation</u>

Occasionally we find ourselves in a more extreme situation; one in which we have serious concerns about our future. Perhaps our contingency plan isn't yet in place and we've learned of imminent layoffs, or perhaps we're in a job we find wholly dissatisfying but haven't yet put ourselves in a position where we're capable of making a change. In cases like these we need a more extreme method to keep a healthy attitude while still maintaining our commitment to excellence.

Situations come and go; sometimes we're the hero; sometimes we're not. Whichever's the case, we should keep in mind the temporariness of the situation. When things have suddenly turned bad we can sometimes forget this and fool ourselves into thinking we're trapped. We need to remind ourselves that no matter how bad things seem, they're not going to stay that way forever, or rather we're not going to let them stay that way forever.

Circumstances go from good to bad and back to good all the time. It's a seesaw of ups and downs and we can't allow ourselves to dwell on the downside when an upside might be just around the next corner. Sometimes a down period can seem uncomfortably long however, and if we ever get to the point where we believe there can be no more upsides, then it's time to create new opportunities. If we're in a situation where we'll have to stay in an uncomfortable position for a longer period than we'd like, we might find it useful to remind ourselves that the job itself doesn't define who we are, but rather it's our personal commitment to excellence that does. More than ever we also need to remind ourselves of the temporariness of the situation.

It's just a paycheck; but an important paycheck

When we've decided to stay in a less than ideal situation for any period of time, it might be helpful to consider the job as just that; a job. Let it be just a paycheck; nothing more. It's the payment we require to put up with a job that doesn't excite us or fulfill us to the extent we deserve or demand in our career. When considering a job as just a paycheck, we almost immediately feel some sense of relief in terms of the stress we're under. Pressure becomes more manageable when we remember that we're being paid to face it and when a job is just a job, it's easier to detach emotionally from what otherwise could be stressful situations.

More than just a paycheck however, it's likely to be an important paycheck that we need to sustain our standard of living and get us by until we can get our career moving in a direction more aligned with our personal goals and priorities. Reminding ourselves of its importance allows us to stay committed to doing our best and not back away from our commitment to succeed. Just because we've taken the attitude that it's just a paycheck doesn't release us from our commitment to excellence or of being extraordinary at what we do. By viewing a situation that's just not right for us as nothing more than a temporary source of income we release ourselves from the stress we're experiencing and increase our ability to directly face the pressure around us. It's a method of remaining dedicated to high performance without allowing the company to become essential to our personal success or self-worth.

The worse that can happen is I lose my house

Another tool to use when things get really bad is to think through the worst case scenarios and set our attitude such that we'll be capable of accepting the situation should it come to be. One of the more extreme examples is finding yourself in a position where you believe there is a real possibility of losing your job. Few, if any of us can be fully prepared for an event like this and it can be an overwhelming and extremely stressful situation. Rather than letting the pressure build to the point we're panicking, we need to realistically think through what might happen and then prepare ourselves mentally and emotionally to the best extent possible. This takes courage but if we can mentally accept the worst case as just a temporary inconvenience and know that we'll be fine in the long run, we'll be much better off.

Things are never as bad as they seem. If we do lose our job, we'll survive. We might go through a tough period but we'll make it. As long as we have a life dedicated to being extraordinary and achieving personal success, we will get there. Opportunity will come and we'll ultimately find something better and more fulfilling. Being able to talk ourselves through and accept these situations helps free us from what could otherwise be high levels of anxiety and stress. Of course the more prepared we are for an event like this the better and this will be the main subject of the next part of this book.

Use bad situations to drive towards our optimal career

We should always be looking for opportunity and sometimes a bad situation can be a great opportunity to move ourselves in a better direction professionally. One realization we should come to terms with is that if we dread going to work every day then we need to make a change. Persistent unhappiness or lack of satisfaction in our work isn't something we need to settle for, nor should we. Persistent unhappiness is a sign we're in the wrong job or working for the wrong company and although it's fine to accept this as a temporary situation, we should make a dedicated and persistent commitment to find something that suits us better. Even while pursuing a change in our career however, we must remain committed to performing our current job in an extraordinary manner. We need to remember that being extraordinary is something we do for ourselves, not for our employer. So even if our employer doesn't acknowledge it, or possibly even deserve it, we remain extraordinary for our sake; because it's who we are.

Part 4

<u>How to Be Extraordinary</u>

<u>with no Job Security</u>

Make Yourself In-demand

Drive your career toward your chosen destination

If you could do anything with your life, what would it be? For some, this question has an obvious answer but for others it's one that requires a great deal of thought. Your ideal career might not be and in fact probably isn't, the one your currently in. Many times we end up on a career path that just sort of happens. Rather than driving our career to a chosen destination, we're more like a passenger going along for a ride; just observing what goes by rather than taking control and steering it in the right direction. Too much is at stake to let our career be left to chance; to let our happiness depend so heavily on external factors.

In some ways there is no single ideal career for us but rather ideal traits that make up and create our ideal job. Ideal traits are those aspects of our work that give us fulfillment, satisfaction, and an overall sense that we're doing a job worth doing. Traits are not the job itself nor are they confined to a particular career path. The same person, doing the same job, in two different work environments can result in two very different levels of satisfaction and fulfillment.

We need to ask ourselves two questions: what is our ideal career and, what is our ideal work environment? To answer these questions we need to take a close look at where we are and beyond to where we'd like to be. We form answers by letting our priorities guide us and by considering what we like and dislike about our current situation. Sometimes our likes and dislikes can be at odds with each other. For example, you might love a challenge but not like the idea of having to put in a lot of extra hours to solve it. When we find a contradiction between what we want and what we don't want, we look deeper to determine a balance that will lead to a personally rewarding career.

There's no right or wrong answers to these kinds of questions; there's no ideal blend of traits that can be generically defined. Knowing what's important to you allows you to guide your career to a better, more fulfilling destination. Having a feel for what drives you and satisfies you, gives a point of reference on which to base decisions about your future. Decisions that if made consciously can lead to a happier place.

Finally, when it comes to getting to your chosen destination; slow and steady wins the race. It's not how fast you get there; it's knowing you're moving steadily in the right direction. Once we determine our chosen career and the traits that make it ideal, we put ourselves on a path to get there. Patience and persistence is required. Although we'll need to set realistic goals, we must also honestly keep track of our progress and never lose sight of the journey.

Be essential to the company's success without allowing the company to be essential to your success

Our goal is to be dedicated to our personal success and by doing so, support whichever company we're working for in achieving success as well. We shouldn't confuse the order. We remain dedicated to helping a company achieve success but we don't do so at the expense of our own. By committing ourselves to becoming extraordinary, we rise above mediocrity and create a standard of performance that is centered on excellence. We take responsibility for our success no matter what the outcome and by doing so, allow ourselves to maintain high performance even under extreme pressures or circumstances where the company's future is uncertain.

Once we form the mindset that our personal success is not inextricably tied to the success of the company we work for, we free ourselves from the stress that often accompanies working for a company where our future is uncertain. We avoid feeling trapped in situations where we have little influence. We come to an understanding that the company we work for doesn't define who we are but in fact that we and our fellow coworkers define the company. We come to an understanding that if this job doesn't work out for whatever reason, we'll use it as a stepping stone to get closer to where we want and deserve to be.

Forming the mindset to do this is the first step, but in order to really free ourselves we have to put certain countermeasures in place. The remainder of this section outlines what those countermeasures are. They take time, effort, and a dedicated persistence but with each step forward you'll find yourself more resilient to the pressures around you; with each step, you'll find yourself more in control of your future; with each step, you'll find yourself closer to an ideal career that's based on what's most important to you. Take the time to plan and implement these steps now. These aren't the kinds of goals that are achieved overnight but as days pass and as months pass you'll find yourself much more in control of your future and your success.

Chapter 15

Invest in Your Skills

We shouldn't leave our experience to chance. To be successful in finding a career that's fulfilling and satisfying requires proactive work to gain the experience we need to get there. Once we have a chosen career, we determine the essential skills required to excel in that career and invest in them. Investing in them assumes developing them, but also goes further. We'll need to be able to show on paper that we have those skills before we'll ever get the chance to show them off first hand. To do this, seek relevant experience, no matter how small or insignificant it might seem at the time. Actively look for opportunities and grab them if they can be used to develop the skills and experience needed to take it to the next level.

For example, a technician who wants to grow into a technical lead position should grab any opportunity to take a lead role even if the task itself is small or low profile. If the company you work for offers training opportunities, try to focus them on something that will help the company but also help you personally and professionally. Write down and keep track of each thing you do that can be leveraged later on to give support for you having the skills needed for your ideal career. If you're not getting the opportunities at work, get them elsewhere. Take some classes on your own or join some groups that are relevant. It's not enough to choose your ideal destination, you're going to have to consciously drive yourself in the right direction if you're actually going to make it.

* Chapter 16 *

Build a Financial Cushion

<u>Start and maintain a rainy day fund</u>

If you were to suddenly lose your job, having a cushion to fall back on can be the difference between high stress and calm focus. You should target to be able to get by for at least six months without having to dip into your retirement fund; a year is better. The economy has its ups and downs and we never know what outside factors could influence our ability to secure a new job. We might also have extra restrictions like not wanting to leave the area we currently live in, that could further increase the amount of time needed to find a good job. With this in mind we should prepare for worst and be ready to spend at least six months out pounding the pavement.

To figure out how much savings is enough you'll need to estimate your monthly burn rate by comparing the minimum amount of spending you can live on, to the amount of revenues you'll have coming in. Things to consider essential are keeping up with your house, car and utility bills as well as a reasonable allowance for monthly food and gasoline expenditures. If you want to keep some additional luxuries then you need a higher savings base to accommodate them. You should also include an allowance for health insurance that you'll have to pick up the cost for when you're unemployed. You can do a quick internet search to estimate Cobra insurance cost. The last time I checked it was about $1400/month for a family of four. Your total monthly expenditure is the combined total of these essential items:

Monthly Expenditures = House payment + car payment + utility bills + food bills + gasoline costs + insurance cost + anything else you want to include.

Your total monthly revenue will be equal to the amount of unemployment compensation you receive plus any side income stream you might have. The day you lose your job, you should apply for unemployment compensation. It can take a few weeks before you get a check so you need to do it right away. You can estimate the amount of unemployment you'll receive by searching the internet for an unemployment compensation calculator. Don't be surprised when you find it's far less than your current take home wages.

Monthly Revenues = Unemployment compensation + other revenue streams

The number you really care about is your monthly burn rate. This is the difference between the expenditures and the revenues and will be equal to the amount of money coming out of your savings account each month. You can use this to calculate the amount of savings you need for your rainy day fund as follows:

Rainy day savings target = 6months * (Monthly Expenditures – Monthly Revenues).

You might get a rude awakening at just how much money you should have tucked away for an emergency. The point is that if you don't have it, then start saving. Make a persistent effort to add something to the fund every paycheck until you reach the full amount. Having a rainy day fund available when you need it could be the difference between losing and keeping your house as well as your sanity if you find yourself suddenly out of work.

Let your vacation build up

Another potential addition to your savings is accrued vacation time. The rules on this differ by state so you'll need to do a quick web search to find out the details for where you live, but many states require a company to pay an employee for their accrued vacation time when employment ends. Even if your state doesn't require it, your company may have an internal policy of paying accrued vacation as a source of severance pay. If this is the case, you should consider doing without much of a vacation for a year or so and letting your available vacation time build up. Once you get a base of a month or more then you can start taking vacations again. A good strategy is to let your vacation time add up to the maximum allowable amount per your company policy and then take a week off; then let it build again followed by another week off, and so on. For example, if your company allows a maximum of six weeks of accrued vacation, then let yours add up to six weeks and then take a week off.

Then wait until it adds up to six weeks again and take another week off. If your company is going to pay you for your accrued vacation time as a form of severance pay, keeping it high eases some of the burden of having to boost up your savings account.

However you choose to build your rainy day fund, do it relentlessly and keep it as a hands-off investment. Don't let yourself be tempted to dip into the fund in order to splurge for a vacation or new toy. Having the fund available does wonders for giving you peace of mind. Having peace of mind allows you to face situations of a possible job loss without feeling the stress that you would otherwise experience.

Consider auxiliary incomes

Finally, to help build a financial cushion and avoid the pain of suddenly finding yourself out of work, consider setting up an auxiliary income. Having an employed spouse of course has its advantages, but what I'm referring to is setting up a side revenue stream for you. This could be an occasional side job related to the field you're currently working in or it could be something totally different. If you have a hobby you're passionate about, consider developing it to the point where you can bring home at least some income from it; no matter how small. Having an auxiliary revenue stream in place can do more than soften the blow of losing your job; it could end up being the impetus for a new career. Necessity is the mother of invention and if you've set up even the most modest alternative revenue stream, it can help overcome any mental obstacles you might have for finding new sources of income.

Chapter 17

Have an Executable Job Find Plan

Have a polished set of resumes ready to send

An executable job find plan is one that's ready to be implemented on a moment's notice. If you find yourself suddenly out of a job you need to be ready to move into action immediately. This is not the time to be forming a strategy on how to go about looking for a new job or be spending time updating your resume. Everything should be in place and ready to go including a good list of candidate companies and individuals to contact.

The first item to have ready to go is a solid resume, or more likely, a solid set of resumes. Keep your resumes fully up to date and spend 20 minutes once a month reading over them. This does two things: first it allows a constant polishing process that after a little time, results in a top notch summary of your skills, experience, and career goals; secondly, it acts as a reminder of what your skills really are. Reminding yourself of what you say you can do reinforces a firm focus on the skills you should be bringing to your current job. This helps keep your perspective focused on being the best professional you're capable of being.

A good resume should include two parts: proof positive of the skills and experiences you've gained throughout your professional career, and a focused statement about moving into a specific job type or function. Because there will likely be more than one job type that your skills and career goals can accommodate, you should have more than one resume available to send. For example; if you have management experience, you could have versions of resumes that specifically list your career goal to be an engineering manager, technical manager, or project manager. The resume you send will depend on which one best matches the job description you're applying for. The body of the resume that includes your skills and experience will remain mostly unchanged, but you should highlight the most pertinent experience to the specific job or role you're interested in.

In addition to having resumes that match your current skills and experience, you should include at least one stretch resume that goes beyond what you've done in the past. For example, someone with management experience might have a version of a resume targeted at a Chief Operating Officer or VP role; someone who has managed small tasks might have a stretch resume targeted towards a project manager or program manager; a technician might have a stretch resume targeted towards being a lead technician or senior technician. To be fully prepared to execute quickly on finding a job, we should have 3-5 or even more versions of our resume polished and ready to go.

Create a strong network of professionals

When it comes to finding a new place of employment, the old saying that "it's not what you know, it's who you know", is more true than ever. Whether we build contacts the old fashioned way with business or index cards, or through sites such as LinkedIn, we want to have a long list of resources ready to help us find new and better opportunities. When it comes to building a network, the more contacts we have, the better. Career opportunities often come from unexpected sources so it's more advantages to spread a wide net than to focus on just a few top notch professionals.

We should think of building a network as a game in which the person with the most points wins. The number of points we get for each contact depends on the value of that contact. For example, a friend or acquaintance that's not involved in the industry we're interested in might count as one point, whereas someone in the same field as us might count as 10 points and someone working at a company we're interested in working for might count as 20 points. To win the game, we not only get as many contacts as we can, but we focus them around industries of interest, companies of interest, or by the strength of the person's own network.

We should constantly be on the lookout for new contacts and set a goal to add a few more to our network each week. Each time we meet someone we should be considering the value this person might bring to our network. Even if it's a brief encounter it's worth getting a business card or sending a LinkedIn invitation. We never know where our next opportunity will come from or how urgent our situation might become, so it's far better to be over prepared than under.

Keep an updated list of companies that you might be interested in working for

In addition to having a strong network of people to contact when looking for a career change, we should also build a strong list of companies we would be interested in working for. This is especially true if we have a very specialized skill set or would like to target a specific geographic area.

Just as with our network of people, we want to have a long list of potential employers mapped out well before we need them. We should create and maintain a running list of companies that we can contact immediately if our work situation suddenly changes; companies we believe our skills would add value to and that we'd enjoy working for. If possible, identify a person at each company that can be contacted directly. If this isn't possible, just having the company identified is a great step in the right direction.

In order to build a large list of potential work places, set aside some time specifically for finding companies of interest. Sites such as LinkedIn or popular job board sites can be great tools for identifying companies of interest. The search engines on these sites allow you to search by specific job function as well as by geographic location. Use these to identify companies you might be interested in working for.

Keep an updated list of recruiters that specialize in your field

Spend some time creating and maintaining a list of recruiters that specialize in your field and that are located in your geographical area of interest. Directories of recruiters can be found on the web or can be purchased from sites like Amazon and others. Simply type in "directory of recruiters" into Google or Amazon's search engine and look through the results. You can narrow down your search by including your field or area of interest: "directory of executive recruiters", directory of technical recruiters, directory of green job recruiters, etc.

To pull it all together, start a folder that includes your polished resume set, network list (if not using LinkedIn), potential company list, and specialized recruiter list. Having all these resources in the same location will make building and updating them convenient and easy to do. Once started, spend an hour or so a week building the different resource lists. A small investment in time will get a top notch list in the matter of a few months. This will be extremely valuable if you ever find yourself suddenly needing to find a new place of employment.

Part 5

<u>Wrap Up</u>

* Chapter 18 *

Summary

Here's a recap of sound bites and one sentence statements that capture the essence of this book.

How to Be Extraordinary

- Don't settle for mediocrity in your life or in your work
- Treat people decently
- Invest some energy to meet the people you work with
- Be interested in the opinions of others
- Give respect as your default position
- Give opportunity to others
- Stand up for your team
- Be honest with yourself and others
- Don't shy away from difficult conversations
- Give praise sparingly; give thanks frequently.
- Take responsibility and give credit when it's due

- Have a collaborative spirit but know when to call it off and be assertive
- Project quiet confidence
- Be at ease with yourself
- Convey believable optimism
- Maintain a calm focus
- Understand what the end point is and what goal you're trying to achieve
- Expect to be surprised along the way
- Manage your mood
- Enjoy your work
- Be in the now; look to the past; drive to the future
- Say what you do; do what you say; have it done when you said it would be

How to Be Extraordinary Under Pressure

- Recognize when stress starts build
- Learn to detach from the pressure without detaching from the job you need to do
- Know your real priorities
- Use your priorities to manage stress

- Keep things in perspective
- Don't transform an unexpected event into a crisis
- Learn to step back from the situation and refocus
- Be a cold blooded professional
- Be neutral to the pressure but not to the people or the result you're after
- You're here for one reason: to get the job done.
- Don't take anything personal
- Lead by example
- Emotional energy is contagious
- Challenge gives meaning
- Recognize burn out
- Know your people
- Overcome resistance to change
- Don't get mentally trapped by a temporary situation
- It's just a paycheck; but an important paycheck
- Think through, and be prepared to accept worst case scenarios
- Use bad situations to drive towards your optimal career

How to Be Extraordinary with no Job Security

- Make yourself in-demand
- Drive your career towards your chosen destination
- Be essential to the company's success without allowing the company to be essential to your success
- Invest in your skills
- Build and maintain a rainy day fund
- Let your vacation build up
- Consider an auxiliary income
- Have an executable job find plan
- Have a polished set of resumes ready to go
- Create a strong network of professionals
- Keep an updated list of companies you'd like to work for
- Keep an updated list of recruiters that specialize in your field
- Spend an hour per week updating resources

Here's to your future
Good Luck!